I0471055

Quick Guide IV: A Scorecard that Accounts for Mindfulness in Business

A simple product and process for CEOs, programme managers and anyone wishing to visualise and measure personal, team or corporate success

Number 4 in a series of articles by

Paul C Burr PhD

http://paulcburr.com/

Acknowledgements

Romilla Ready, Lead Author, *Neuro-linguistic Programming for Dummies®*

Steven Howard, Digital Marketing Strategist, Website SEO Writer, Marketing Consultant at *Howard Marketing Services*, Greater Los Angeles

Kristen Johnson, Learning and Development Professional

Other Titles in this Series

Quick Guide: How Top Salespeople Sell

Quick Guide II: How to Spot, Mimic and Become a Top Salesperson

Quick Guide III: How to Bridge the Pillars of Successful Business Relationships

Other Titles by the Author

Defrag your Soul

2012: a twist in the tail - a novel

Learn to Love & Be Loved in Return

Contents

Preface

This article, in common with each of my other *Quick Guides to Business*, can be read quickly in less than an hour. It's also a workbook which you can go through at your own pace to complete the exercises included.

The contents bear from my research, consulting, direct selling and coaching within global corporations over a twenty year period. The companies I worked directly for, or in a freelance capacity with, include: IBM, Cisco, Accenture, Xerox, American Express, Standard Chartered, BP and Reckitt Benckiser. During this period I've had the privilege to meet and work with hundreds of top performers worldwide.

When I use the phrase 'you', I mean you, me, us, we, your team or your organisation.

Paul C Burr, July 2013

.

Summary

Mindfulness Scorecard

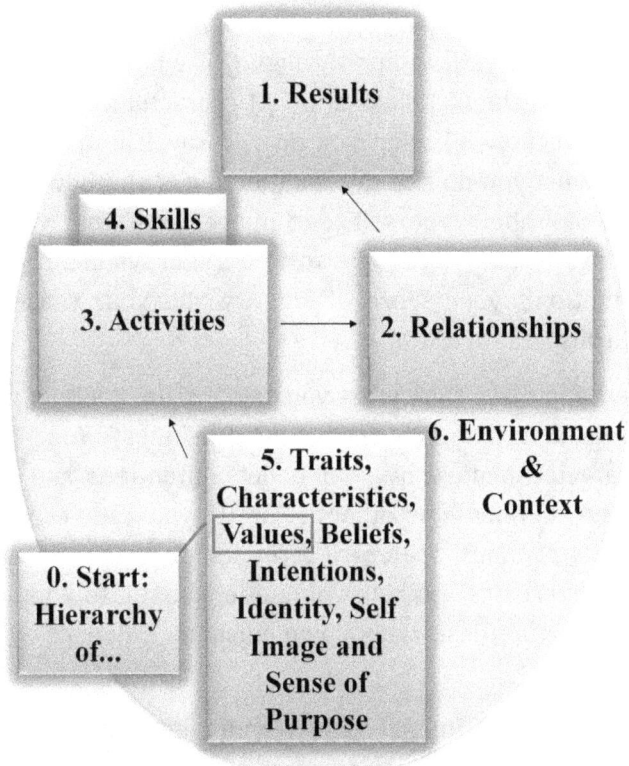

When I first 'pieced together' the *Mindfulness Scorecard*, I called it, *"The Dashboard for Success"*. I did so because it illustrates the metaphorical 'jigsaw pieces' required to succeed where most people do not; 'the what and how' top performers differentiate themselves from moderate performers; the 'what and the how' of what top performers do to feel good which 'moderates' find less easy to do.

You achieve (1. - refer to *Mindfulness Scorecard*) results through superior (2.) business relationships. You forge these (2.) relationships through (3.) what you do and say - and the (4.) skills and (5.) character with which you execute (3.) what you do and say. The quality of (3.) what you do and say is a function of (5.) how good you feel about yourself (self image) and what you're doing, what's important to you (your values), your intentions, your sense of identity and your sense of purpose.

Perhaps more than what you say and do, it's how you come across to others that matters most. Your (5.) character, shaped by your beliefs, intentions and self image, defines how others relate to you and respond. The *Mindfulness Scorecard* accounts for your traits and characteristics - to help you guide yourself to winning ways with those whom you wish to influence with integrity.

Healthy self-image: when you feel good about yourself and what you're doing, you will 'go the extra mile' to forge key business relationships you need, in order to succeed. You demonstrate passion and enthusiasm. You create the (6.) environment and shape the 'human context' (i.e. the governing values and beliefs of stakeholders) to succeed.

When you feel not good, you may find yourself giving 'second best' to these relationships; you undervalue yourself and what you have to offer. You need to be mindful; be who and do what you need to feel good.

Top performers (whether they're executives, managers or professionals) are very, very mindful about the results and outcomes they wish to achieve. They visualise the picture, hear the sounds and/or sit in the feeling of success before it happens. They know intimately where they are (the present moment) and where they want to be (a future moment) - yet not necessarily how they will bridge the gap between these two.

(Author's note: moderate performers don't find it as easy as top performers to imagine success.)

These two respective sets (of imagery, sounds and feelings), of the 'now' and the 'future', are all top performers require initially to invoke the *Law of Business Attraction* - see chapter of the same name in *Quick Guide II: How to Spot, Mimic and Become a Top Salesperson.*

As you read this guide you will discover why feeling good is paramount - and how to feel better, if not good, about the most challenging people and situations you face - including yourself. And once you are mindful - you are better positioned to start and remain feeling good! I intend to write more on this latter subject, *staying mindful*, in my next *Quick Guide.*

A good place to start, to determine what success means to you, is to bring into focus what's important to you. When you place all the things that are important to you in priority of order, you have fleshed out your (0.) *Hierarchy of Values.*

(0. Start:) Hierarchy of Values

Refer to *Mindfulness Scorecard* illustration.

Bring to mind a project you're engaged, or are about to become engaged, in. Write its name on the top of a blank sheet of paper. Write down answers to every question or instruction that follows, written in italics.

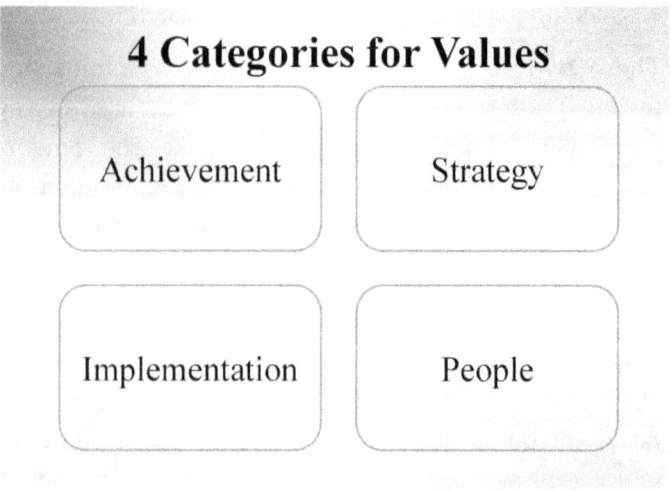

As you think about the project, what's important to you? List your thoughts and place each in one of four categories...

1. ***Achievement*** - e.g. financial results, measurements, market share, facts, logic, scientific/statistical analyses
2. ***Strategy*** - e.g. 'global/big picture', positioning, leadership, long term, entrepreneurship
3. ***People*** - e.g. stakeholder buy in, relationships, passion, trust, truth, warmth, caring, integrity, security of mind, resonance, buy in
4. ***Implementation*** - e.g. activity planning, project management, compliance, governance, step-by-step approach, risk reduction.

Read through each category. Take a step back and be mindful of all your answers.

How balanced are your answers?

What's missing?

What would you like to add (if anything) to any category to achieve a sense of balance between them?

Make a note of any conflicts (e.g. achievement versus people considerations, risk reduction versus entrepreneurship)?

Prioritise the four categories (Achievement, People, Strategy and Implementation) in order of importance to you.

_____

Case Study: European Energy Corporation

I coached the European General Manager of a well known energy firm who was charged with reshaping the company's proposition from a product supplier to a services provider. Although achieving the transformation on time and within budget was very important to my client, he was not prepared to engage in the transformation without the collective approval/buy-in of the National General Managers (specifically, Germany, UK, France and Italy).

He prioritised his values accordingly and decided that in terms of categories, his priorities were:

I. *People* - specifically, their 'passion, commitment and buy-in' to the transformation project.
II. *Strategy* - specifically, a shift in market identity and value proposition as a services provider by 'top tier' customers
III. *Achievement* - business growth in services' business
IV. *Implementation* - completion of transformation project, to plan, on time and within budget.

We achieved this by my client answering the following iteration of questions.

Can you achieve II (change in market identity) without I (people's commitment and passion) in place? Answer: *"No".*

Can you achieve III (growth in services revenue) without II (change in market identity by top tier customers) in place? Answer: *"No".*

Can you achieve IV (timely completion) without III (growth in services' revenue) in place? Answer: *"Yes and No".*

My client felt that even if the project didn't deliver the results on time, it was more important to take a customer centric approach to achieving a growth in services' revenue i.e. growth will come from how top tier customers identify with and value his company as the "best services provider".

Although budgetary constraints and timeframes were important, my client remained mindful that the appropriate change in customer perceptions and expectations would be the 'pull' that would determine the project's success; more so than the efficacy of how well the project plan was put into action - the 'push'. So he placed category III (Achievement) slightly ahead of category IV (Implementation) whilst remaining mindful that the two categories went hand in hand.

(End of Case Study)_____

With your list of categories (of 'what's important' criteria) prioritised - you have effectively created your personal *Hierarchy of Values* for the project. There are no rights and wrongs. Each stakeholder you deal with may well have a differing *Hierarchy of Values* and you will need to 'tune-in' to what their *hierarchy* is, in order to influence them - see *Quick Guide III: How to Bridge The Pillars of Successful Business Relationships*.

Being mindful of your *Hierarchy of Values*, let us now paint *your* picture of what success will look like. Move to box *1. Results*, in the *Mindfulness Scorecard*.

_____

(1.) Results

Refer to *Mindfulness Scorecard* illustration.

Imagine your project succeeds completely. In your mind, move forward in time. Go straight to the project's successful outcomes and sit in the feeling of having achieved exactly what you wanted to achieve. *Imagine and feel!*

Now answer...

- *What financial results or other measures have you achieved?*
- *What other tangible outcomes have you achieved?*
- *What new wisdom have you or others acquired? How can you apply that wisdom?*
- *What new power have you unearthed?*
- *How are other people responding to you?*
- *What will your success enable you (or your organisation) to do next?*

Tier 1 Analytical Thinking:

This level of thinking creates the intellectual or analytical answers you come up with to the aforementioned questions.

Tier 2 Thinking and Feeling:

As you scan the answers to the above questions, raise your thoughts 'up a level'. Allow your mindful thoughts about each of the above 'elements of success' to transmute into feelings. One by one, sit in the feeling(s) of each 'element of success'. (You are already, in part, invoking the *Law of Business Attraction*. The stronger your ability to imagine the feeling of success, the stronger the passion you project, the stronger your 'magnetic pull' for success - see *Quick Guide II: How to Spot, Mimic and Become a Top Salesperson*.)

3 Tiers of Thinking & Feelings

Tier 3 Thinking & Feeling:
Aggregate Feelings

Tier 2 Thinking & Feeling:
Thoughts become Feelings

Tier 1 Thinking:
Analysis and Intellect

Tier 3 Thinking and Feeling:

Combine all your feelings into an aggregate feeling of success. Allow a 'sense of passion' to fill your whole body, a *passion for wisdom and truth*. Rise up to a *third tier* of thinking and feeling. Without forcing it, gently 'brighten the colours', 'turn up the volume' and 'intensify the feeling'.

The longer you sit in this third tier, or *meta-position*, of thinking (*meta* is derived from Greek, meaning *above, beyond*), the more intense you allow the feeling to be within you and the more frequently you allow this meta-feeling into your whole body (not just your head) - the stronger the vibe you project to those around you.

Power (of thought and feeling) = Duration x Intensity x Frequency (of passion for wisdom and truth)

First and foremost, a *passion for wisdom and truth* is what attracts other key stakeholders to your way of thinking and being. As you sit in this 'meta-feeling' place it to one side and now develop your passion for the *journey* to success. A *journey* that is fundamentally about the acquisition and application of wisdom.

The *journey* is more than a metaphor for life itself. Life is the *journey*, is life. Top performers are equally passionate about the *journey* as they are about its successful outcome. They are equally passionate about the acquisition, sharing and application of *wisdom and truth* with others.

A *passion for wisdom and truth* (amongst other key traits and characteristics) forms the basis for (and thereby differentiates them from 'moderates') how top performers forge business relationships - see *Quick Guide II: How to Spot, Mimic and Become a Top Salesperson*.

———

(2.) Relationships

Refer to *Mindfulness Scorecard* illustration.

You achieve results only through relationships, first and foremost through the mindful relationship you have with yourself - to which we shall return later. Bringing your mind back to the present moment, be mindful of where your project is right now. Imagine a radar screen with a light beam that sweeps in a circular motion around its centre. *Blips* appear on the radar screen. Each *blip* represents a relationship you have with a stakeholder in your project.

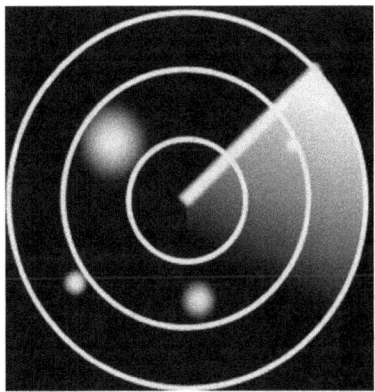

Image courtesy of *http://openclipart.org/*

The larger the *blip*, the more important the relationship is to the project's success. The largest *blips* represent the relationships you have with those who have the *power of veto* over the project's success. These are your *top-priority* relationships. The remaining *blips* represent people who have an interest in or some influence over the project's success. Be mindful primarily on the largest *blips*, the *top-priority* relationships.

As you focus on each of the *top-priority* relationships, notice how bright its *blip* is. A pure white light indicates your relationship with this person is exactly where you want it to be in order for you both to achieve success. If it's kind of half way between light and dark then it's neutral or perhaps the other person is undecided about their commitment to the project's success or to you. If it's dark or very dark then you may have some resistance to overcome.

Be mindful of the size and brightness of each of the *top-priority blips*. Find somewhere peaceful, close your eyes, take three deep and slow regular breaths, count to 4 on the in-breath, pause for a moment, and count to 4 on the out-breath, and pause again. Now allow your breathing to become shallow and regular.

Visit each *top-priority blip*, one by one. On each visit, imagine shining a light into it. Answer/perform the following (Write down your answers and learning so that you give your mind a chance to be mindful.):

- *What's important about this relationship to the other person? And to you?*
- *What's important about the project to the other person? How does that contrast with what's important to you?*
- *What are the key background facts that determine each blip's luminescence? What feelings does each of these facts evoke in the other person? And in you?*

- *What does or will the other person want from you? Is there anything that you would need from them first or in return?*
- *Imagine giving and receiving what's needed to the relationship to brighten its blip so that it becomes a pure white light (or at least much brighter).*
- *What's one word or phrase that describes the relationship when it's exactly how you want it to be? That is, the blip is filled with pure white light. (Examples of clients' phrases include: mutual trust, respect, energised, caring, considerate and so on.)*

Repeat the above for each *top-priority* relationship and others that your intuition guides you to consider. Take a step back and be mindful of any conflicts you might need to resolve between people.

Success can be reframed as a network of collaborative business relationships. When everyone who can stop you is 'on board', there is no one else to stand in your way (i.e. only you can stand in the way of your own success - see *values & beliefs,* later). Ergo you will succeed.

Your task is to illuminate each *blip* as much as you can so that it, ideally, becomes a pure white light.

———

(3.) Actions and Behaviours (with Passion and Enthusiasm)

Refer to *Mindfulness Scorecard* illustration.

You forge relationships partly through what you do and say. The action of giving and receiving in the previous section demonstrates your contribution to each relationship; it demonstrates your *relationship to the relationship.*

Relationships with others are challenging when you allow them to invoke anxiety and apathy in you. You give or receive 'second best.' In each case, rather than focusing on your relationship, focus on your 'relationship to the relationship' first; release the anxiety and apathy.

When you choose to give or receive 'second best' - you would be essentially undervaluing yourself. When your *relationship to the relationship* is second best that's what you'll probably receive, 'second best'.

If you want something from the other party in a relationship, e.g. candour or honesty, you might choose to...

- Give what you want to yourself first, i.e. be candid and honest with yourself first, and act on the intuitive answers you give yourself (inner wisdom)
- Give what you want to the other party first, i.e. express candour and honesty with them

- Ask for what you want directly, in this case, candour and honesty

Or

- Demonstrate a passion and enthusiasm for what's important to the other person without asking for anything in return, i.e. in accord with their hierarchy of values - and do so regardless of what or how the other person responds. This is not about making yourself into a 'door mat'; it's a genuine experiment to improve the relationship objectively and with integrity. Your commitment (i.e. relationship) to the relationship remains intact regardless because you've detached yourself from the responses you get.

For example, I recall a conversation with a *General Manager of African Countries* of a multi-national energy company. He had a passion to unite three nations economically (South Africa, Egypt and Nigeria) to lead the emergence of Africa as a prosperous continent. The large investment that the company I worked for was making in those nations grabbed my client's attention and as a result he was always keen to understand how our business in those countries fared. His door was 'always open' to anyone from my company wanting to see him. This wasn't a deliberate act on my behalf to forge the business relationship I wanted with the *General Manager* but it does illustrate the collaborative response you can get when contributing to something seen as very important to the person you're dealing with, without asking for anything in return.

No matter which of the above or other strategies you take to influence your client (with integrity), your *passion for wisdom and truth* and your *relationship to the relationship* remains enthusiastic.

———

(4.) Skills and Competencies - The Science of Influencing and Other Important Factors

Refer to *Mindfulness Scorecard* illustration.

The act of giving and receiving will hone your influencing skills. Practising the strategies in the previous section is only the first level of the much wider topic of 'influencing skills' which is beyond the purpose of this book.

Briefly it includes...

Develop your *Sensibility* - one of *7 key traits* top performers demonstrate that 'moderates' do less so.

(Extract from *Quick Guide II - How to Spot, Mimic and Become a Top Salesperson*)

Sensibility

When you feel sorry for someone you sympathise. When you share your understanding of another's feelings you empathise. My definition of sensibility goes beyond empathy; to describe an awareness and responsiveness to the intellectual (logic) as well as the mental and emotional position a client takes. Top salespeople have a profound ability to stand in the client's shoes to the extent that they can say to themselves, *"If I were the client, I would take the exact same actions as they are taking".* This is not sympathy or empathy, it is awareness of how, where and why the customer sees things differently to the salesperson. (After all, if they had the exact same views as you, you wouldn't need to do any selling.)

Business text books (I've come across) reason that two people have different perspectives about something because they followed different logic to get where they are, or they started from a different place. But differences of opinion go beyond the intellectual.

They will have differing levels of fear - especially about the unknown. They will both possess subconscious counter intentions [ergo, they can't articulate what holds them back). They will have different preferences (e.g. big picture or attention to detail; achievement before people or vice-versa; a scientific (facts, logic reason) or intuitive ('gut feel') approach].

Sensibility is the 'sense + ability' to stand in the client's shoes and use the appropriate logic and language patterns they prefer; thereby making a connection at intellectual, mental and emotional levels.

(End of extract)

Prepare to be at your peak, in every key meeting you have.

Top performers do three essential things to be at their peak (for a fuller understanding refer to *Quick Guide II - How to Spot, Mimic and Become a Top Salesperson*)...

1. **Clarify your outcomes** for the meeting in hand and how you want the relationship with the person to develop, meeting by meeting, one step at a time. Moderate performers focus less on the latter dimension.
2. **Be mindful of the frame of the mind you want to be in** and that any meeting (is hopefully a meeting of minds) is ultimately about helping everyone present to frame a congruent viewpoint of what needs to be done.
3. **Prepare your strategy, primarily so that you allow yourself to get in the frame of mind you want to be.**

Research I've come across and my own experience shows that the most important thing you take into a meeting is your frame of mind followed by being clear about the outcomes you seek. Having a strategy is important but, once the meeting has started, it's factors '2' and '1' above (and in that order) that will determine most how you 'handle any curve balls thrown your way'.

Influence people who, at first, don't wish to be influenced

This is the most advanced form of influencing you'll have to deal with. Looked at another way, when you influence the most difficult people you meet then influencing everybody is a relatively straight forward task.

The task involves giving yourself a larger number of influencing strategies. Some, perhaps most, will be 'off your radar'.

They're off your radar because you attach some form anxiety or apathy to the picture of doing them. (We avoid or procrastinate doing things that are important for only two reasons: anxiety and/or apathy.)

The 'trick' is to see/imagine these influencing strategies in action, from a variety of perspectives, before you execute them. Prior - you will need to take an 'inner journey' to elucidate these strategies.

I refer to a Neuro-linguistic Programming (NLP) based methodology by which I help clients to create a number of strategies (passion and enthusiasm) to influence the most challenging people they deal with. (For a quick tool refer to page 110, *Self-Coaching Tip: To Deal with Someone You Have Been in Conflict With*, from *Learn to Love and Be Loved in Return.*)

What else does it take to achieve gravitas with those that you influence?

For a list of skills, competencies and knowledge areas that top salespeople demonstrate when they are with and away from the people they are attempting to influence: refer to *Appendix 1 - Corporate Sales Competencies* of *Quick Guide II - How to Spot, Mimic and Become a Top Salesperson*. The illustration on the next page summarizes these concepts for you.

By and large, the skills, competencies and knowledge areas, illustrated, are not peculiar to the sales profession. They are demonstrated by all top performing influencers in business and everyday life. All are rooted in a passion and enthusiasm for relationships.

Illustration: Sales Competencies At and Away from the Customer Interface

In-depth Knowledge

Applying Technology

Business

Industry

Clients

Clients' Customers

Competition

Self

Gravitas with Customer

Consultative Selling

Coaching & Consulting

Influencing

Skills at the Client Interface

Negotiating

Away from Customer

- Personal Effectiveness
- Account/Territory Management
- Complex Bid Management

Relationship Strategies
- Clients
- Internal Networks
- External Networks

Value Generation
- Knowledge
- Measurements
- Intellectual Property
- Innovation – service and product

Strategic and Analytical Skills

21

(5.) Traits, Characteristics, Values, Beliefs, Feelings and Imagery - Mindfulness

Refer to *Mindfulness Scorecard* illustration.

This topic covers the fundamental 'inner things' about you that will influence how passionate and enthusiastic you are - and if you are willing to go 'the extra mile'.

By 'inner things', I mean traits and characteristics that demonstrate your feelings, emotions, values, beliefs, your sense of identity, your intentions and sense of purpose.

Top performers differentiate themselves by exhibiting *7 key traits...*

1. *Faith-in-self*

2. *Curiosity*

3. *Composure*

4. *Sensibility*

5. *Co-opting*

6. *Inspirational*

7. *Passion*

For a fuller explanation of the above *7 key traits*, refer to *Quick Guide II - How to Spot, Mimic and Become a Top Salesperson.*

Through these *7 key traits* you can create the mindfulness to notice your frame of mind, day by day, meeting by meeting and eventually, minute by minute. You will be mindful (or not) of every relationship you have, especially the one you have with yourself.

Let's go back to your project at hand. Focus on the image of success you've created; the relationships you've forged that underpin that success; the giving and receiving actions you have or will take to strengthen those relationships and the skills, competencies and knowledge areas you've developed and demonstrated. As you encompass all these things in your mind, answer the following questions and perform the following actions...

- *What would you need to believe in or about yourself for your picture of success to become a reality? Sit in the feeling of that belief. If that's difficult then 'act as if' it's a reality already.*
- *What would you need to believe about the project or task in hand for your picture of success to become a reality? Sit in the feeling of that belief. If that's difficult then 'act as if' it's a reality already.*
- *What would you need to believe about each of the key people you're dealing with in order to attain your picture of success? Is that feeling congruent with your passion and enthusiasm to learn to succeed? If not, what would you need to believe or be mindful about the relationship you create with each person? Notice and rise above any conflicts. Allow yourself to induce resolutions to such conflicts rather than deduce any. Be patient, trust yourself. Allow your passion and enthusiasm to attract issues that remain incomplete*

23

and provide you with the wisdom to complete them as they present themselves.

The resolution of the issues is firstly an intuitive process that will provide the insight and information with which you use your intellect to apply in practise.

- *What else would you need to believe about the products and solutions you're proposing, your organisation and its people or the world at large? Use the same inductive, intuitive and then intellectual process to resolve any conflicts.*

It's the passion and enthusiasm you emit that connects you to those things that need completing, to succeed. Passion and enthusiasm breed the creativity to complete what is incomplete. Without passion and enthusiasm you may miss connecting altogether. You deny yourself the roadmap to success.

As you assimilate all the aforementioned facts and feelings, consider the following...

1. *Who are you in this picture of success? What image of yourself do you conjure? (I've had clients who saw themselves as a 'soaring eagle', a 'wise panther', a 'peasant farmer who cultivates barren sales territories!') How does the image of yourself relate to the task in hand? What is it about that image that would encourage you to 'go the extra mile'? So what would you do? Be specific.*

2. *What are your intentions and goals? What wisdom might you assimilate in achieving your goals? What remains incomplete within you?*

3. *Are you allowing any anger, hurt, shame or fear to hold you back? Notice those negative feelings and where they come from... your head, neck, chest, abdomen, stomach or loins. Allow those feelings to be. Neither feed them nor deny them. If you feed them (e.g. you allow fear or anger to take control) you become clouded in emotion; your judgement becomes clouded. If you attempt to repress or deny their existence, you do not have them in your 'possession' to release.*

   Instead acknowledge them, place them in a 'bubble' and leave them be. If anything, imagine shining light into that bubble. Imagine how you would be and feel if you didn't have those negative emotions. Act as if, as best you can, feeling those feelings and being that person - whilst at the same time allowing the negative emotions to float around, untouched, in 'bubbles'.

By remaining mindful, acknowledging your vulnerabilities without interfering with them, you'll find that they eventually 'get bored, and leave'. This can take time. For deep rooted issues, it can take years. Yet when they leave, despite feeling real at the time, you discover their illusory nature. I plan to write a further booklet that will go into the topic in some depth.

———

(6.) Context and Environment - Self Coaching Exercise

Refer to *Mindfulness Scorecard* illustration.

Create the context for success by completing everything you've started or promised to do. Do the most important things first. They are often the most onerous. This enables you to focus your energy on the success of your projects by having no 'incompletions' hanging around in your head - especially those that create the most apathy or anxiety in your psyche.

Study the context of the people you wish to influence. (I refer you also to a powerful self coaching tool, *Raising Passion and a Sense of Security (in others)* in *Quick Guide III - How to Bridge the Pillars of Successful Relationships.*)

Notice how the context and environment in the picture of success differs or has changed from the as-is-now picture.

As you look around make a list or mind map of all the important contextual and environmental factors that may have an impact on or will be impacted by your project. For example...

- Market segment or industry: political, economic, sociological, technological, environmental issues, something else?
- Your customer, your own company, your competitors: customer activity, finance, business drivers, key performance measures, business

processes, products and solutions, information systems, use of technology, something else?

- Your own personal: working conditions and methods, incentive schemes, training, equipment, finance, support services, something else?

As you scan the list, make a note of the 'top three' factors that will enable your success and the 'top three' factors that will inhibit success. Write down how each of the three enabling and three disabling factors might aid or thwart success.

Give each factor 'the CIA (Control, Influence or Accept) test'. Mark each as a C, I or an A.

C - Is it controllable?

I - Can I influence (i.e. increase or lessen the likelihood) this factor? or

A - Do I have to accept that it is not realistically under my control (e.g. economic upturn or downturn)?

According to each enabling factor's C, I or A designation: how could you go about accelerating, increasing, or preparing to utilise its impact?

According to each disabling factor's C, I or A designation: how could you go about preventing (head off at the pass), avoiding (circle around), remedying (heal or make whole), contingency planning for or defending against its impact?

By working through all the hitherto exercises in this guide, you now have a fully fleshed out picture of what success will look like and hopefully have connected many (unnoticed) 'dots of the unknown'. With the metaphorical jigsaw complete you can put together a more informed plan of action.

Before you put your plan into action, it's worth noting some of the dynamics that come into play and how to avoid emotional setbacks when things don't work out the way you expect or desire, the first time around.

———

The Dynamics of two 'S-words', Success and Setback

I try to remember not to use the *f-word*. Many people associate it with an unwanted ending or a finality - whereas the word 'setback' implies that all is not lost. Whether you use the *f-word* or not, 'all' is never lost. There always exists 'learning'.

Let's start with the first of two *s-words*, 'success'. When you win a huge sales contract or business campaign, you feel good about yourself. You feel motivated, confident, competent and hopefully curious to learn and apply more wisdom - to create more success. You're willing to 'go the extra mile'.

[Ref: *Effectiveness = Motivation x Confidence x Competence x Curiosity (E=MC³)* from *Quick Guide II - How to Spot, Mimic and Become a Top Salesperson.*]

When you 'go the extra mile' (beyond your competitors), you forge better relationships. The better the relationships you forge, compared to your competitors, the more success you enjoy. And the cycle of success continues until, one day, you don't get the success you set out to achieve. You attract a setback.

If you allow the disappointment or hurt from not achieving success into your psyche, you might become less confident. When you're less confident that can affect your motivation or you may feel less competent. If you're in a highly political environment, for example, you may want to hide 'mistakes' (un-learning or un-application of wisdom) made. You sweep them under the carpet for fear of being perceived as incompetent or singled out from those around you as an 'underperformer'.

When you're feeling down and it affects your self-esteem, you're less likely to 'go an extra mile that involves some form of risk'. You don't forge relationships as strongly as perhaps you desire. You know what happens next. You plunge yourself into a downward spiral.

The 'trick' is to build a 'firewall' between the results you achieve and the feelings you allow yourself to feel. You only allow one thing to pass through the firewall... 'self-acknowledgement'.

Acknowledge = Accept + Congratulate + Reward + Consolidate Learning

Specifically, you don't allow any blame in the form of anger, hurt, shame or fear through the firewall.

Keep Anger, Shame, Hurt and Fear at Bay

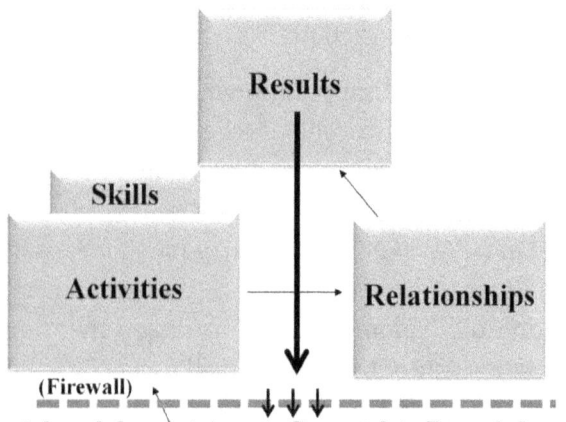

Acknowledging success is a bit of a 'no brainer' yet the same process applies to its alternative. Accept a setback for what is, an opportunity to learn that which remains incomplete. Congratulate and reward yourself for the input you've put into the project and your willingness to learn. Sustain that willingness; apply the wisdom learnt; to hopefully figure out not only *what to do differently* but perhaps more importantly *how to be different* next time and complete what is incomplete.

Failure is only failure when you think of it as the end result in any process.

Romilla Ready, Author, *Neuro-linguistic Programming for Dummies*

(Pardon the *f-word*!)

———

Concluding Remarks

I'll complete the main body of this *Quick Guide* by providing you with a reframe that's taken me some time to work through. It's adapted from druidic wisdom (ref: *Light and Life*, a series of booklets written by David Loxley, *Chief Druid, The Druid Order*, London).

Your purpose is more than to succeed. It is to learn and apply the wisdom needed to succeed.

Success is the goal, but life is the time and space that happens in between now and reaching that goal. You attract the future that comes towards you. The future presents you with what remains incomplete right now in your life. Should you complete what is incomplete, it travels into the past and need not return.

Whatever travels into the past that remains incomplete 'returns to the future'. Whatever issues (i.e. unlearned or unapplied wisdom) that remain incomplete, be they business or personal, return again and again until you complete them.

When you start something, complete it.

(End of main body of article)

———

Thank you...

...For purchasing this article.

I plan to write further business articles in this *Quick Guide* series. Continuing the theme of *mindfulness*; the next article has the working title, *Quick Guide V: Mindfulness in Business Relationships.*

If you'd like further information about the variety of services I engage in, please visit these websites:

http://paulcburr.com/ ~ extensive and ethereal blog-site that combines business and ancient wisdom

http://www.facebook.com/PaulCBurr ~ over 16,000 followers

http://twitter.com/paulburr

www.cotoco.com ~ for 'wisdom- transfer' solutions; to pass on what the top performers in your organisation do differently from the 'moderates'

Or mailto: doctapaul@paulcburr.com

Appendix 1: Comparisons with Other Frameworks and Scoring Systems

5 Measures of Learning

The *Mindfulness Scorecard* encompasses Fitzpatrick/Phillip's widely-used, five levels of measuring the effectiveness for training interventions[1].

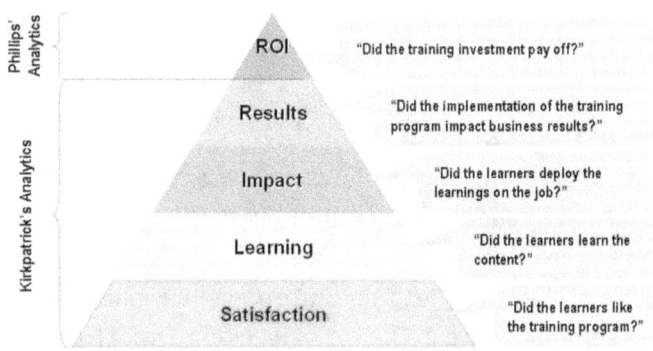

---

[1] Ref:
http://leanlearning.wikispaces.com/learning_analytics#kirkpatrick-phillips_model

(Illustration sourced under Creative Common Licence from Aptech, *http://leanlearning.wikispaces.com*)

Satisfaction - level 1: is covered by *Traits, Characteristics, Values, Beliefs, Feelings...* (and rather than happy, the focus is on the passion and enthusiasm to learn)

Learning - level 2: What wisdom have people learnt?

Impact - level 3: How are they applying that wisdom? What are people doing differently or more of?

Results (from Relationships) - level 4: Measures the *"So what are people feeling and experiencing differently in their business relationships with you and one another?"* question

Return on Investment - level 5: Results - are you getting what you set out to achieve?

Neurological Levels Model

The scorecard encapsulates the (six) *Neurological Levels NLP Model*, created by Robert Dilts[2], one of the world's leading NLP luminaries. Dilts was inspired by Gregory Bateson[3], leading anthropologist, philosopher and seminal figure in the early development of NLP.

---

[2] Ref: *Tools For Dreamers – Strategies For Creativity And The Structure Of Innovation* and *From Coach to Awakener*
[3] Ref: *Steps to an Ecology of Mind*

Inspired by Dilts, I added a further level to his model, namely *Traits and Characteristics* to make seven levels.

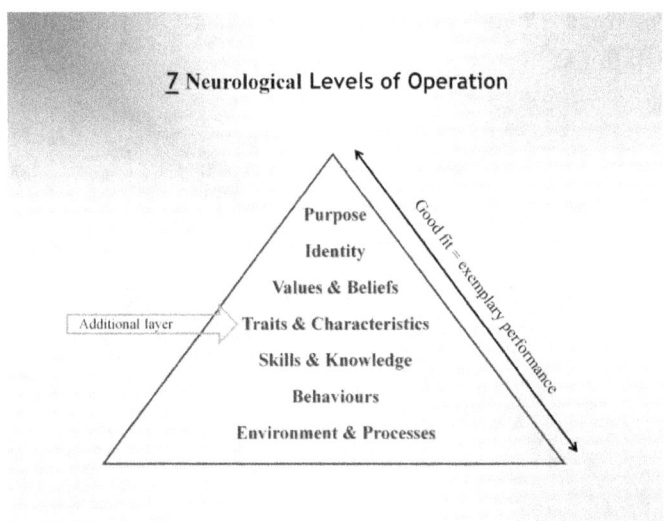

Notice, in the model, that real change occurs in you when your higher levels of operation change, namely your sense of purpose, identity, self-imagery, values and beliefs. Others will often infer these tacit inner feelings you have from the traits and characteristics you demonstrate to them (the 'how you come across') - and the 'what you say and do'.

Balanced Business Scorecard

The *Mindfulness Scorecard* also embraces Kaplan & Norton's *Balanced Business Scorecard*[4] of the causal relationships to model business success.

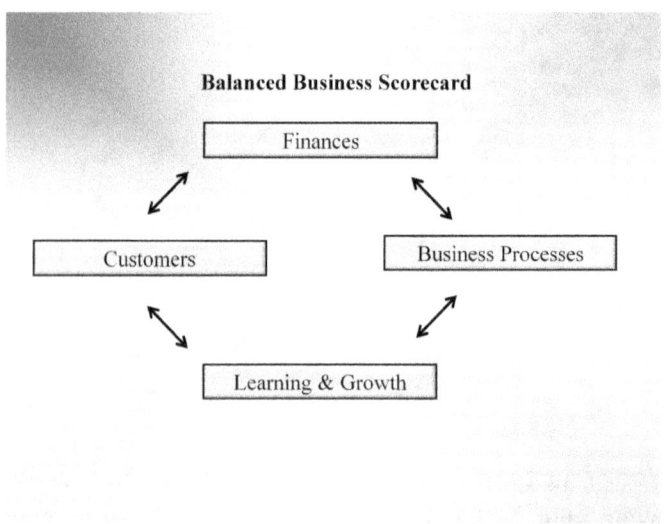

Financial Results - corresponds with *Results*

Processes - corresponds with *Environment and Actions & Behaviours*

Customers - corresponds with *Results and Relationships*

Learning and Growth - corresponds with *Actions & Behaviours*

---

[4] ref: *The Balanced Scorecard: Measures that Drive Performance, Harvard Business Review*, 1992, Jan – Feb pp71-80

The *Mindfulness Scorecard* would appear to encompass all the above systems and frameworks on a single page, provided it's large enough!

———

Appendix 2: About me, Paul C Burr

Photo © Stephen Cotterell

I equip people to improve their effectiveness by 30%+ in a matter of weeks, sometimes days.

Business Client: *"I have worked with Paul periodically over the past 8 years to gain solutions to a number of people issues / opportunities. If you are looking for a Personal Coach to make a High Performer / High Performing Team even better (particularly a senior player) – I would not hesitate to recommend him."* - Sandra Ventre, Management Development Director, Reckitt Benckiser (now with Qantas)

Private Client: *"You have been so instrumental in the positive changes in my life, I set quite a few goals, and one by one my goals are being achieved, thanks*

to you, showing me how." - Debbie (via Skype) Cape Town, South Africa.

The Skills and Passions in Me

Life doesn't get better by chance; it gets better by change.

And change is a journey that's two parts emotional to one part intellectual.

Most of us don't achieve what we set out to achieve at the first attempt. If the outcomes you sought were down to a purely intellectual exercise then you would have achieved them already - would you not? Whether you're a top or moderate performer (or underperforming right now) - every change you make in life is a journey, two parts emotional to one part intellectual. We are twice as likely to hold ourselves back because of self-imposed limiting beliefs we hold about ourselves, our organisation or customers, as opposed to intellectual problems. Put simply, I equip people to tackle challenging emotional journeys; to go beyond the limits to success they impose on themselves and others.

Corporate clients use me as a 'business coach', personal clients probably see me as more of an 'energy healer'. In both cases I help clients to cultivate and apply their innate willpower, imagination, courage and creativity to achieve the business and personal outcomes they seek.

I have over thirty-five years of B2B corporate sales and management experience, sixteen years of which overlap with my business and personal coaching work. I have a PhD in Statistics and a First Class Honours Degree in Mathematics. I'm qualified as a Master Practitioner in NLP, this/past life regression and hypnotherapy.

I give talks (and appear on talk shows) on selling, executive coaching, Neuro-Linguistic Programming (NLP), ancient wisdom, football and more ethereal subjects – sometimes to the same audience!

I write books, blogs and am now partway through a series of business articles based upon my own original research, experience and observations in corporate and small/medium sized businesses.

I study and practice ancient wisdom, astrology, casting runes, dowsing, the I Ching and the Tarot.

I love listening to music – rock, jazz, country… you name it. I sing a bit too.

I'm a passionate football fan of Newcastle United Football Club, in "Geordieland", in The North-East of England.

My Promise:

The material I use is powerful, very powerful. I know of nothing quicker or more effective. It's non-mainstream - which means you get non-mainstream results.

The Author in Me

Quick Guide - How Top Salespeople Sell

"...a must read for both novice salespeople and the experienced...." - Chiahou Zhang, author

"I loved it... it was great. I've encouraged many of my directors to buy a copy as it's very pertinent to my company" - paraphrased from a top performing B2B salesperson for a global IT Services organisation

"I work for a large American IT company, and can say this is a hugely powerful book to articulate what is required to get to Board level. To really understand what the CEO and C level executive

summarise as valuable and impactful, and in a condensed easy-to-digest format, is phenomenal. I find Paul C Burr's style of writing easier to digest and apply in any sales situation; it crystallises where the true business value add is delivered and how you really have strategic partnerships. I have just got number 2 book and look forward to reading this with excitement - which is saying something as my concentration span can be limited. Thank you." - Amy Lambkin, Amazon review

Quick Guide II - How to Spot, Mimic and Become a Top Salesperson

Quick Guide II:
How to Spot, Mimic
and Become a Top
Salesperson

(for new or seasoned
sales professionals,
managers and CEOs)

Number 2 in a series of
articles by

Paul C Burr PhD

Quick Guide III - How to Bridge the Pillars of Successful Business Relationships

Quick Guide III:
How to Bridge the
Pillars of Successful
Business
Relationships

(for CEOs, salespeople
and everyone in between)

Number 3 in a series of
articles by

Paul C Burr PhD

Learn to Love and Be Loved in Return

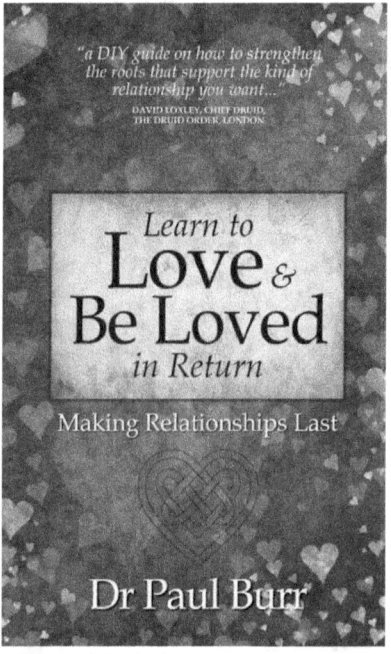

"Uplifting: this is one of those books that arrives in your life at just the right time, when you need it most. The author is able to convey a very deep and meaningful message in an easy to read and understand format with a step by step guide on how to achieve this. The best type of love is unconditional and what better place to start than with yourself." - Rhedd, Amazon review

2012: a twist in the tail, a novel with spiritual insights

"This is a compelling story for our troubled times. Paul C Burr writes with passion and compassion about moral uncertainties and the quest for salvation and spiritual fulfilment. Go with the flow, trust your inner-self and enjoy this humane and optimistic tale." - Professor John Ditch, York, UK.

"This is a gripping read - beautiful, insightful and very enjoyable. I found phrases and thoughts staying with me, and becoming part of my understanding of the world." - Caroline Eveleigh, *Getting to Excellent*

Defrag your Soul

"You should be proud of DYS Paul. I think it is amazing and I'm still thinking hard about what you've written." - Amanda Giles, author

"DYS whispered to me, 'take heart, be aware, let your journey this far nourish your inner self to be at peace, to love and to shine as your journey continues'." - Penelope Walsh, book review

www.ingramcontent.com/pod-product-compliance
Lightning Source LLC
Chambersburg PA
CBHW072029190526
45166CB00015B/1424